Can Science Solve?

The Mystery of Atlantis

Holly Wallace

Heinemann
LIBRARY

First published in Great Britain by Heinemann Library
Halley Court, Jordan Hill, Oxford OX2 8EJ
a division of Reed Educational and Professional Publishing Ltd.
Heinemann is a registered trademark of Reed Educational & Professional
Publishing Limited.

OXFORD MELBOURNE AUCKLAND
JOHANNESBURG BLANTYRE GABORONE
IBADAN PORTSMOUTH NH CHICAGO

Designed by **AMR** Ltd, Bramley, Hants, England
Printed in Hong Kong

04 03 02 01 00
10 9 8 7 6 5 4 3 2 1

ISBN 0 431 01646 1

This title is also available in a hardback library edition (ISBN 0 431 01641 0)

British Library Cataloguing in Publication Data

Wallace, Holly
  Atlantis. – (Can science solve?)
  1.Science – Methodology – Juvenile literature 2.Atlantis –
  Juvenile literature
  I.Title II.Wallace, Holly
  001.9'4

  ISBN 0431016461

Acknowledgements

The Publishers would like to thank the following for permission to reproduce
photographs: Ancient Art and Architecture Collection: p11, R Sheridan pp8, 18, 19,
G Tortoli pp16, 20; Fortean Picture Library: pp7, 10, K Aarsleff p13, J and C Bord
p22, W Donato pp25, 27, Llewellyn Publications p24; Ronald Grant Collection: p5;
Oxford Scientific Films: R Packwood p14; Science Photo Library: p6, D Parker p12;
Still Pictures: C Guarita p28.

Cover photograph reproduced with permission of Ronald Sheridan, Ancient Art
and Architecture Collection.

Every effort has been made to contact copyright holders of any material
reproduced in this book. Any omissions will be rectified in subsequent printings if
notice is given to the Publisher.

Any words appearing in bold, **like this**, are explained in the Glossary.

Contents

Unsolved mysteries

For centuries, people have been puzzled and fascinated by mysterious places, creatures and events. Is there really a monster living in Loch Ness? Are UFOs tricks of the light or actually vehicles from outer space? Who is responsible for mysterious crop circle patterns – clever hoaxers or alien beings? Did the lost land of Atlantis ever exist? Some of these mysteries have baffled scientists, who have spent years trying to find the answer. But just how far can science go? Can it really explain the seemingly unexplainable? Are there some mysteries which science simply cannot solve? Read on, and make your own mind up...

This book tells you about the **legendary** lost land of Atlantis, from the only account that exists of the city, written by Plato in the 4th century BC, to later theories about its supposed location and the geographical, **archaeological** and historical theories about its existence and destruction.

What was Atlantis?

According to legend, Atlantis was an ancient island **civilization** in the Atlantic Ocean which flourished about 12,000 years ago. Then, in the space of a night and a day, it sank without trace beneath the waves. It was a powerful kingdom, whose army had conquered large parts of Africa and Europe, before being defeated by the Ancient Greeks. Its people enjoyed a **privileged** lifestyle, surrounded by fine things and beautiful palaces. Until one fateful day, that is, when their golden world came crashing down around them.

4

But did Atlantis ever actually exist? We have no eyewitness reports to go by. No ruins have ever been found. Apart from one ancient account, later theories have often been based more in science fiction than in science fact. And if Atlantis did exist, two burning questions still remain – where was it located and how was it finally destroyed? Was it a natural disaster or an act of the gods? Is there anything science can do to solve one of the greatest mysteries of all?

Many books and films have been based on the story of Atlantis, including this one, entitled The Lost Kingdom. This is a scene inside the fabulous royal palace of the Atlantean king.

5

Beginnings of a mystery

The first and only sources we have for the mystery of Atlantis are two ancient accounts, written by the Greek **philosopher** Plato in the 4th century BC. They are written as imaginary conversations which take place between the philosopher Socrates and three friends. The two accounts are called *Timaeus* and *Critias*, after their main characters. Plato began to work on a third account but it was never completed.

Plato, the Greek philosopher, who lived from 428–347 BC. The legend of Atlantis began with his ancient accounts. But were they historical fact or merely hearsay? No one knows.

Two accounts

In his version of events, Plato puts the story of Atlantis into the mouth of the poet and historian Critias. He says that he heard the story as a child from his grandfather, who had heard it from his own father. He, in turn, had heard it from his friend Solon (c640–558 BC), a famous Greek politician from Athens who had been told the story by an elderly Egyptian priest. By the priest's time, the story was already very old, recorded in the ancient temple records. It tells how, about 9000 years before Solon's birth, or about 12,000 years ago, Atlantis was a rich, powerful island in the Atlantic Ocean whose armies conquered many of the lands around the Mediterranean until they were finally defeated by the Athenians. This is Plato's account of the Egyptian priest's words:

6

'There was an island situated in front of the **straits** which you call the Pillars of Hercules (now called the Straits of Gibraltar) and which was larger than Libya and Asia Minor (modern Turkey) put together... . Now on this island of Atlantis there was a great and wonderful **empire** which ruled over the whole island and several others, and over parts of the **continent**, and controlled, within the straits, Libya as far as Egypt and Europe as far as Tyrrhenia (Italy). This vast power attempted to **subdue** both my country (Egypt) and yours (Greece) and the whole region within the strait. Then, Solon, your country defeated the invaders and saved us all from slavery. But afterwards, there occurred violent earthquakes and floods, and in a single day and night, the island of Atlantis was swallowed up by the sea and disappeared...'

A map of Atlantis from the 1644 book, Mundus Subterraneus [The Underground World], by Dutch writer Athanasius Kircher. He based his guess at Atlantis' location on Plato's accounts.

7

What was Atlantis like?

In his second account, *Critias*, Plato described the history, geography and people of Atlantis in more detail. He tells how the kings of Atlantis were created by Poseidon, the Ancient Greek god of earthquakes and the sea. They were great architects and engineers, building temples, palaces and harbours. Their capital city was circular in shape and built on a hill, surrounded by alternate rings of land and water which were joined by huge bridges and tunnels. A huge canal connected the outermost ring of water to the sea. Behind the city was a great, fertile plain where farmers grew the city's food. The island was also rich in minerals, timber and exotic animals, including elephants.

According to legend, the people of Atlantis were descended from the sea god, Poseidon. Atlantis took its name from the giant Atlas, one of Poseidon's sons.

An artist's impression of the gardens of the magnificent palace of the King of Atlantis. But did it really exist?

A magnificent palace

According to Plato, the priest told Solon how the King of Atlantis lived in a luxurious palace on top of the hill. In the centre of the palace stood a temple to Poseidon. This is how Plato describes it:

'The outside of the temple was covered in silver, apart from the **pinnacles**. The pinnacles were covered in gold. Inside, the roof was made of ivory, decorated with gold, silver and other precious metals. All the other walls and pillars were lined with precious metals. In the temple they placed golden statues – there was Poseidon himself standing in a chariot pulled by six winged horses, and of such a size that he touched the roof of the temple with his head...'

It seemed the Atlanteans had everything they could wish for. But, says Plato, they became greedy and corrupt. Zeus, the king of the gods, decided to teach them a lesson and destroyed their golden land as punishment.

But even 50 years after his death, doubts began over whether Plato's Atlantis was a real place. Had the story truly been passed down to him as he claimed, or had he invented it in order to discuss the politics of his own city, Athens? Was the account historical fact or hearsay? The debate continues today.

9

Interest renewed

Modern interest in Atlantis began in the 19th century with the publication, in 1882, of an extraordinary book called *Atlantis, the **Antediluvian** World*. Written by an American politician, Ignatius Donnelly, the book quickly became a best-seller all over the world. The cult of Atlantis was born.

Donnelly's theory

Donnelly firmly believed that Atlantis had existed and that it had perished exactly as Plato described. He placed the island in the Azores in the mid-Atlantic (see page 16) and argued that he had 'several distinct and novel propositions' to back up his theory.

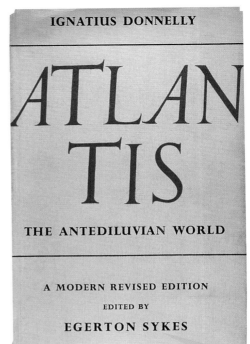

The cover of Donnelly's best-selling book, Atlantis, the Antediluvian World. *It sparked off a huge amount of interest in the mystery of Atlantis.*

This is what he claimed:
- A large island, Atlantis, once existed in the Atlantic Ocean. It was all that remained of an Atlantic continent.
- Plato's description was historical fact.
- **Civilization** itself began in Atlantis.
- Atlantis was a mighty power which conquered many other countries.
- It was the true antediluvian world.
- The oldest colony founded by the Atlanteans was in Egypt.
- The Atlanteans were the first people to use iron and bronze.
- The Atlanteans invented the first alphabet.
- Atlantis was destroyed by a natural disaster, such as an earthquake or volcanic eruption.
- A few people escaped on rafts and ships.

10

A lack of evidence

Donnelly based his theories on his reading of Plato's account of Atlantis and in his own study of a variety of sciences, including **zoology** and **geology**. In the 19th century, these 'new sciences' were beginning to be studied and taken seriously for the first time. His claims captured the imagination of a great many people but serious scientists dismissed them as nonsense. After all, there was no hard evidence whatsoever to back them up.

Sun worship

*From his study of ancient religions, Donnelly concluded that the people of Atlantis worshipped the Sun and that their religion spread to Ancient Egypt and Peru. Since then, **archaeologists** have discovered many Egyptian paintings showing worship of the Sun god, Ra, and mysterious carvings of the Sun in the Nazca desert in Peru. Could Donnelly's claims be true?*

This Egyptian painting shows the Sun god, Ra, travelling in his solar barge between Nut, the sky goddess (above), and Geb, the Earth god (below).

11

Other theories

Although many people dismissed Donnelly's book as pure speculation, it sparked off a massive amount of interest in Atlantis. Thousands of books, articles and short stories followed, and the name of Atlantis was used on everything from ships to a region of the planet Mars. There were hundreds of other theories too, some based, if loosely, in science; others completely made up. Here are just some of them...

This huge crater in Arizona, USA, was formed when a giant meteorite hit the Earth some 50,000 years ago. Could an even larger meteorite have caused Atlantis to sink?

Bombardment from space

Several theories suggest that Atlantis was destroyed by an enormous **meteorite** hitting the Earth. In 1976, German scientist and engineer, Otto Muck, published his book *The Secret of Atlantis*. In it he points to two huge depressions, 7 kilometres deep, on the sea floor in the western Atlantic, as likely **impact craters**. Scientifically, this could have been possible – in 1920, a meteorite weighing 59 tonnes struck Namibia in Africa, the largest meteorite yet known. But Muck calculates that the Atlantic meteorite must have been 10 kilometres wide and claims that it also split the Atlantic Ocean open along the line of the Mid-Atlantic Ridge, a long chain of underwater mountains running down the middle of the Atlantic Ocean. Science has since proved this to be untrue (see pages 16–17).

12

Evidence from eels

In his book Muck also suggested that the sinking of Atlantis could explain the mysterious **migrations** of eels across the Atlantic. Each year, European eels leave their river homes and swim across the Atlantic to the Sargasso Sea to breed. Then the tiny **elvers** begin an incredible 6000-kilometre, three-year-long journey home, carried on the warm waters of the Gulf Stream current. Muck wondered why the eels should risk such a long and dangerous journey?
He suggested that the Gulf Stream once circled Atlantis and carried the eels to fresh water by a much shorter, more direct route. When Atlantis sank, it broke the flow of the Gulf Stream and made the eels' journey much longer.

Pyramid parallels

*Some people, including Lewis Spence, a writer from Scotland, tried to link Atlantis to the **civilizations** of Central and South America. Between the 1920s and the 1940s, he wrote several books pointing to similarities between, for example, the pyramids built by the Mayas in Mexico and those built by the Ancient Egyptians, whose country was supposedly ruled by Atlantis. But many historians do not believe that the two are linked. They occurred independently in each place.*

A Mayan pyramid in Mexico. Because it was similar in shape to the pyramids of Ancient Egypt, supposedly a colony of Atlantis, Spence suggested that its building may have been influenced by Atlantean culture.

Atlantis found?

So, if Atlantis did exist, where was it located? According to Plato, 'it was an island situated in front of the **straits** which are called the Pillars of Hercules'. This places it to the west of the Straits of Gibraltar (called the Pillars of Hercules by the Greeks) in the Atlantic Ocean. But not everyone agrees. Some of the alternative locations suggested for Atlantis include America, Scandinavia, the Canary Islands and even Greenland. You can read more about possible locations on the following pages.

Lost in the jungle

The English explorer, Percy Fawcett, was convinced that Atlantis lay in Brazil where **archaeologists** were already beginning to rediscover the ancient ruins of long-lost cities in the jungle. In 1924, he set off to find it. His belief was based on a stone statue he had been given, which he was sure came from Atlantis. He was never seen again. Rumour said that he had been killed by a local chief, or that he had found his lost city and liked it so much he did not want to leave.

The summit of the Rock of Gibraltar. In ancient times, this rock and Mount Hacho, in modern Morocco, were known as the Pillars of Hercules, marking the division between the Mediterranean Sea and the Atlantic Ocean.

St Brendan's Isle

In the Middle Ages, many people believed in the existence of mysterious islands in the Atlantic Ocean. These were called 'paradise islands' because they were thought to be perfect, unspoilt worlds. The islands were marked on medieval maps and many voyages were undertaken to find them. One of these, St Brendan's Isle, was discovered by St Brendan, an Irish monk, in the 6th century AD. Some people have identified these islands with Atlantis.

Northern Europe

In his 1976 book, *Atlantis of the North*, German scholar, Dr Jürgen Spanuth tried to prove that Atlantis was located off the north-west coast of Germany where there was a group of sunken islands. He also claimed that the people of Atlantis were, in fact, the early ancestors of the Vikings. But no evidence has yet been found to support his claim.

Antarctic Atlantis

American author, Alan F Alford suggested in his 1996 book *Gods of the New Millennium*, that Atlantis may have been situated in Antarctica. He says that, at the time given by Plato for Atlantis's existence, which was about 12,000 years ago, Antarctica was ice free. When the region did freeze over, which was about 6000 years ago according to Alford, its people (the Atlanteans) spread far and wide throughout the world, including Egypt where they built the pyramids. It is true that Antarctica was not always a frozen **continent**. It once had a much warmer climate than today. But from the **geological** study of ancient rock and ice samples, scientists know that Antarctica was largely covered in ice two to three million years ago, so Alford's theory could not be correct.

15

Earth movements

In his book (see page 10), Ignatius Donnelly suggested that the likeliest site for Atlantis was the Azores, a group of islands in the middle of the North Atlantic. This theory has now been disproved by **geologists**.

The Earth's crust

The Earth's hard, outer crust is not one single layer of rock. It is split into seven huge, and numerous smaller, pieces, called plates. The plates are constantly floating or drifting on the layer of red-hot, liquid rock, or magma, lying beneath them. This is called continental drift. Usually this happens without anyone noticing. Sometimes though, the plates collide or pull apart violently, causing earthquakes and volcanoes.

An island in the Azores, where Donnelly believed Atlantis to lie. Since then, his theory has been proved to be scientifically impossible.

Mid-Atlantic Ridge

In the middle of the Atlantic Ocean, two plates of crust are slowly pulling apart. Over millions of years, magma has welled up to plug the gap, then hardened and been pushed upwards to form a chain of mountains. This process is called sea-floor spreading. The chain of mountains is the Mid-Atlantic Ridge, the longest mountain range on Earth. It runs down the entire length of the Atlantic, splitting it in two and rising to the surface in only a few places, including the Azores.

16

Disproving Donnelly

Donnelly claimed that the Azores were the mountain tops of a large, sunken island, namely Atlantis. By the time that Donnelly's book came out (1882), the Mid-Atlantic Ridge had been discovered but very little was known about its geology. The modern science of **oceanography** (the study of the oceans) has shown that the Azores are, in fact, islands which have grown up from the sea-bed as a result of sea-floor spreading. They cannot be Atlantis.

Continental drift

*The first person to claim that the crustal plates moved was a German scientist, Alfred Wegener, in 1915. He suggested that, about 200 million years ago, all the land was joined together as one huge continent, called Pangaea. It was surrounded by a vast ocean, Panthalassa. Over millions of years, the plates drifted apart and Pangaea split up, eventually forming the **continents** and oceans we have today. Until the 1960s, Wegener's theory was not taken seriously. Then, geologists discovered that the plates did indeed move. They also found fossil evidence of plants and dinosaurs to support the idea that the continents were once linked, as Wegener said.*

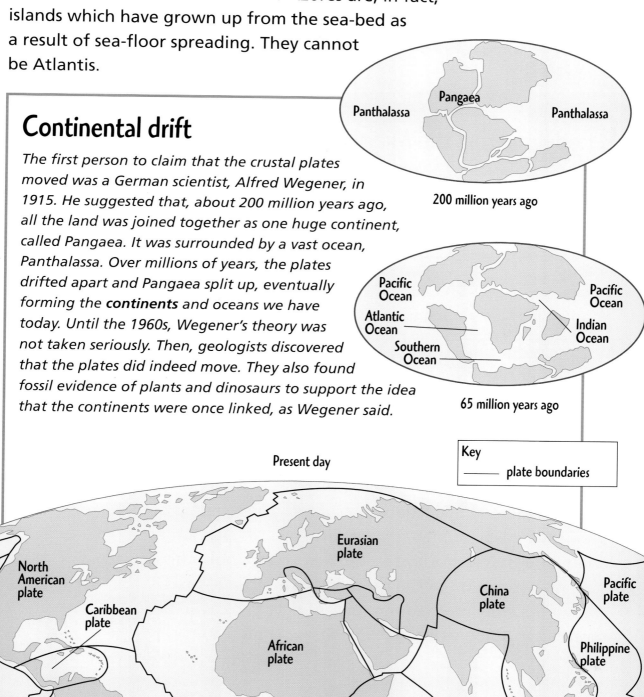

200 million years ago

65 million years ago

Present day

Key — plate boundaries

Looking at the past

One of the most believable theories about the location of Atlantis places it in the Mediterranean Sea, on the Greek island of Crete. It was here, about 4000 years ago, that a mighty **civilization** grew up, which showed many similarities with Plato's Atlantis. Could they be one and the same? Some scientists think they might be.

Part of the ruined Minoan palace of Knossos. Some scientists believe that the Atlanteans and Minoans may have been one and the same people.

Rediscovering the Minoans

*Our knowledge of the Minoans, the people who lived on Crete some 4000 years ago, comes from archaeological evidence found on Crete. In 1900, British **archaeologist**, Sir Arthur Evans, began excavating the magnificent royal palace at Knossos. He uncovered a civilization far more advanced and sophisticated than anything yet found in Europe. Evans called it Minoan after a **legendary** ruler, King Minos.*

Similarities ...

From Evans' discoveries, other scholars drew similarities between Minoan and Atlantean culture. The Minoans built their towns around magnificent royal palaces. The largest and grandest was at Knossos. Did Plato hear about this and base his description of the royal palace in Atlantis on it? Or had the story reached the Ancient Egyptians, who had passed it to Solon as Plato claimed (see pages 6–9)?

18

Evans also found many paintings and sculptures of bulls which were sacred animals for the Minoans. Plato described a similar **cult** of bull-worship on Atlantis.

*A **fresco** from Knossos showing the ancient sport of bull-leaping. Both the Atlanteans and Minoans were said to have worshipped bulls as sacred animals.*

Finally, both the Minoans and Atlanteans met a mysterious and violent end. In about 1500 BC, Minoan civilization was destroyed by a series of natural disasters, including earthquakes and tidal waves. Similar to the 'violent earthquakes and floods' which Plato says destroyed Atlantis...

... and differences

So could Crete be Atlantis? Despite the similarities, there are problems with the theory. Firstly, Crete was not a round island, as Plato described Atlantis to be, and it did not sink beneath the sea and vanish without trace. Secondly, it is not located in the Atlantic. However, Minoan script, called Linear A, found on clay tablets and discs from Crete, has not yet been deciphered by archaeologists. Who knows what secrets it might hold...

A violent volcano

Many experts have linked the collapse of Minoan **civilization** to the violent eruption of Thera, a volcanic island about 110 kilometres to the north of Crete. Or could Thera itself have been Atlantis?

Excavations at Akrotiri on Santorini (Thera) have uncovered a great city in Minoan style. Could these be the long-lost ruins of Atlantis?

Thera erupts

The traditional date given for the eruption of Thera is 1450 BC, about the same time as the Minoan collapse. So violent was the explosion that most of Thera was blown away, leaving only a small, crescent-shaped island which is now also called Santorini. This may have caused tidal waves, flooding and earth tremors on Crete. Recent **archaeological** evidence suggests, however, that Thera may have erupted some 200 years earlier and may not have been responsible for the destruction of Minoan Crete. Even if these two dates matched, they still placed the destruction of Atlantis just 900 years before Solon, not 9000 as Plato claimed.

20

Thera as Atlantis

So, could Thera have been the **catastrophe** which destroyed Atlantis? Greek **archaeologist** Professor Spyridon Marinatos certainly thought so. He also believed that Thera was linked to Crete, possibly as a result of the spread of Minoan culture throughout the Mediterranean. In 1967, he began excavating at Akrotiri, in the south west of Santorini (Thera). Buried under layers of volcanic ash, Marinatos found the remains of a great city, with streets of Minoan-style houses and **frescos** showing a highly advanced civilization. As for the problem of dates, outlined above, he suggested a scribe responsible for recording events had simply written the wrong dates down, multiplying everything by ten.

Another possibility is that Thera itself was Atlantis. After all, scientists know that, during the eruption which destroyed the island, the central part of the island sank into the sea.

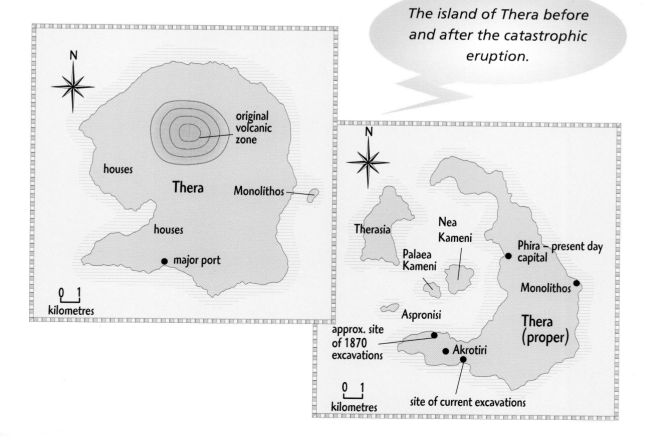

The island of Thera before and after the catastrophic eruption.

Other sunken cities

Atlantis-hunters have not given up hope of finding their lost land. After all, they argue, there are many other examples of ancient places which have been rediscovered, thousands of years after sinking beneath the sea. They include the ancient Greek port of Apollonia in Libya which was built in about 630 BC, and Port Royal, the pirate city described below. One day, the ruins of Atlantis may be among them.

Lost kingdom

A group of rocks called the Seven Sisters lies in the sea, about 10 kilometres off Land's End, the southernmost tip of Britain. According to legend, they mark the site of a kingdom which once linked Britain to France. It was called Lyonesse. In the 5th century AD, a huge wave swept over Lyonesse and it disappeared beneath the sea. There was only one survivor. Since then, local fishermen have hauled up many fragments of buildings and other objects in their nets. They claim that these come from Lyonesse.

One of the Seven Sisters rocks off Land's End, Cornwall. This was said to be the site of the lost kingdom of Lyonesse which, like Atlantis, sank into the sea.

22

Diving dilemmas

There are many problems with diving to look for ruins. As divers go deeper, the weight of the water pressing down on them increases. This weight is called water pressure. This produces bubbles of gas in their blood. If they surface too quickly, the bubbles cause a painful, sometimes deadly condition, called the 'bends'. To avoid this, divers spend time in a 'decompression chamber' where they slowly and safely return to normal pressure. Of course, some problems are more difficult to overcome than others. Take, for example, this theory of why divers have not yet found Atlantis – namely that, as they dive, they enter another dimension...

Port Royal

On 7 June 1692, the pirate harbour of Port Royal, Jamaica, slumped into the sea. Just before midday, the city was hit by a massive and disastrous earthquake. The whole of the waterfront, complete with streets, houses and shops, slid into the sea. A huge tidal wave swept over the city and, in two short minutes, two thirds of the city had been swallowed up and two thousand people were dead. For hundreds of years, the ruins of Port Royal lay underwater. Then, in 1959, an American ship, *Sea Diver*, specially equipped with **echo sounders** and **radar**, explored the site. Further excavations by divers and **archaeologists** followed in the 1960s. Thousands of **artefacts** were found.

Strange stories

As you have seen, there are many different theories about Atlantis. Some have been very carefully thought out, taking science and history into account to try to solve the mystery. Often, unfortunately, the science used has since been proved wrong. Other theories are much, much stranger, without any basis in science at all. Many have been put forward by people called **occultists** whose interest lies in the world of the supernatural.

TRUE STORIES OF THE STRANGE AND THE UNKNOWN
July 1953 35¢

FATE

HAS ATLANTIS BEEN FOUND?

TELEPATHY IN PETS

MURDER BY A G...

Atlantis rising

Atlantology is the name given to the study, scientific or otherwise, of Atlantis. Many Atlantologists believe that, one day, Atlantis will rise again. This may not mean that the island will physically rise from the sea but that there will be a return of the qualities and virtues of goodness, courage and wisdom which made Atlantis great. The only question is ... when?

*Despite many theories having been disproved, the possibility of finding Atlantis still fascinates both **archaeologists** and those interested in the supernatural.*

The fourth race

In 1877, Russian occultist, Helena Blavatsky published a huge book, called *Isis Unveiled*. It contained just one page on Atlantis. In it, Madame Blavatsky claimed that the people of Atlantis were the fourth 'race' on Earth, a super-human people who lived long before the present human beings, and who had amazing **psychic** powers. But they were corrupted by a great dragon king, Thevetat, and turned into wicked magicians. They began a war which ended with Atlantis being submerged.

In her next book, *The Secret Doctrine*, published after she died, Madame Blavatsky had more to say. The book is a commentary on an ancient text said to have been actually written in Atlantis. Among her many claims, she tells how the survivors of Atlantis settled in Egypt and built the pyramids about 100,000 years ago. But modern science shows that the earliest were actually built in about 2600 BC.

A huge stone statue of a Toltec warrior.

Toltec ancestors

In the 1890s, another occultist, W Scott-Elliott claimed to be able to read the so-called 'Akasic Records'. These were a secret history of ancient wisdom, said to exist on the astral plane, in another dimension beyond normal life. From his reading, he claimed that Atlantis had existed an incredible one million years ago. There were seven races of Atlanteans, one of which was the Toltecs. In conventional history, the Toltecs were a nomadic people of Mexico. They built their capital at Tula, north of Mexico City, in about AD 900.

A false start

In the 1920s, an American **clairvoyant**, Edgar Cayce, claimed that he had spent one of his past lives in Atlantis. According to him, Atlantis reached from the Sargasso Sea to the Azores and was about the size of Europe. Its land and **civilization** had been destroyed twice, in the course of which the mainland had been split into islands. The last to sink was near the Bahamas. In 1940, Cayce predicted that this part of Atlantis would rise again, some time around 1968. But was he right?

Fakes and frauds

*In the 1870s, German archaeologist, Heinrich Schliemann, discovered the ruins of the ancient city of Troy in Turkey, the site of the **legendary** Trojan War. Forty years later, his grandson, Paul, claimed that Troy and Atlantis had been allies. He said that his grandfather had found a bowl at Troy, inscribed with the words 'From King Cronos of Atlantis'. Archaeologists later proved that the bowl was a fake.*

The Bimini Road

Early in 1968, an **archaeologist**, Dr J Manson Valentine, found a J-shaped pathway of rectangular stone slabs about 700 metres long and lying several metres underwater off the coast of North Bimini, in the Bahamas. It became known as the Bimini Road. There was great excitement. Had Atlantis been found, as Cayce had predicted? One Atlantis-hunter had no doubt. He claimed that the stones were part of an ancient Atlantean temple. One of them might even be the head of a stone statue.

Scientists disagreed. Some said that the pavement had been formed naturally. Others accepted that it could be man-made but was likely to be the remains of a sea wall which had sunk beneath the water. In 1981, in the course of an **oceanographic** survey of the area, the US Geological Survey solved at least part of the mystery by proving that the 'Road' had indeed been laid down by natural means between 2500 and 3500 years ago, long after Atlantis.

An intriguing glimpse of the Bimini Road. You can just pick out the J-shaped pathway of stones beneath the water.

In conclusion

So, can science really solve the mystery of Atlantis? It seems, unfortunately, extremely unlikely. We do not even know if Atlantis was ever a real place at all. The only source we have for its existence are Plato's two accounts which report the story as hearsay, already many thousands of years old in Plato's time. Whilst the Ancient Egyptians certainly existed, as did Solon, to whom the story of Atlantis was told, no one knows how much historical fact is included in Plato's accounts. Modern experts generally agree that Plato was in fact talking about his own city, Athens, which had once been rich and powerful, as Atlantis had been, and now faced decline. Perhaps it was intended as a warning to his fellow Athenians not to become corrupt and greedy as the Atlanteans had done.

The great city of Athens, Greece, as it appears today. Was Plato really talking about Athens, not Atlantis, in his famous accounts? If so, perhaps Atlantis only existed in his imagination.

28

Could Crete be Atlantis?

If Atlantis did exist, its likeliest location seems to be the island of Crete in the Mediterranean. The work of **archaeologists** has thrown up many similarities between Minoan culture and that of Plato's Atlantis. And science has shown that Crete was struck by earthquakes and floods, possibly triggered by the violent eruption of nearby Thera. But nobody knows for sure.

Fact or fiction?

In 1975, a special conference was held at the University of Indiana, USA, to debate the question: Atlantis – fact or fiction? A team of experts came to the conclusion that Atlantis was a myth. It is true that there is no solid proof at all. But, of course, even experts sometimes get it wrong!

What do you think?

Now that you have read about Atlantis and the possible theories for and against its existence, can you draw any conclusions? Do you feel that any of the theories can be taken seriously? Do you have any theories of your own? Despite the lack of eyewitness accounts, are we any nearer to knowing the truth?

What about the mysterious Bimini Road? What were the natural means that laid it down? Do you see any merit in the Minoan argument, despite disagreement about the dates? Try to keep an open mind. If scientists throughout history had not continued to investigate the strange or mysterious, many vital scientific discoveries may never have been made. And having no proof is very different to proving something wrong.

Glossary

antediluvian the time before the flood. There are many myths about a great flood sent by the gods to punish people for becoming wicked. Before this, they lived for centuries in peace and happiness in paradise.

archaeologist scientist who studies the past by looking at ancient ruins and remains

artefact ancient object, such as a pot, a piece of jewellery or a weapon, which helps to tell archaeologists about the past

catastrophe a sudden, widespread disaster

civilization a people and the society they live in

clairvoyant a person who claims to have the power to look into the future

continent a large mass of land

cult a religious group

echo sounder an instrument used to measure the depth of the water and to map the features of the sea bed. It gives out pulses of sound which hit parts of the sea-floor and send back echoes. The pattern of the echoes is traced on to a screen to create a picture of the sea-floor.

elver a young eel

empire a large group of countries ruled by one, strong power

fresco a painting drawn on wet plaster

geology the scientific study of the rocks of the Earth's crust

impact crater a deep hollow in the ground left when a meteorite hits the Earth

legendary based on a legend, which may or may not be true

meteorite a lump of space rock which originally comes from comets and which sometimes crashes into the Earth

migration a long journey made by some fish, birds and mammals between their feeding and breeding grounds

occultist a person who is interested in the supernatural

oceanography the study of the oceans. It is a mixture of different sciences – biology, geology, chemistry, physics and meteorology.

philosopher a person who studies the meaning behind life and the Universe. In Ancient Greek times, a philosopher was someone who studied all aspects of the world around them.

pinnacle a decorative turret on a building's roof

privileged lucky or honoured

psychic a person who claims to be able to read people's minds and to see into the future

radar an instrument used to detect the direction, range and presence of objects which show up on a screen

strait a narrow channel connecting two large areas of water

subdue to put down

zoology the scientific study of animals

Index